The
Veggie Burger

Over 30 deliciously healthy recipes for vegetarian and vegan burgers!

By Susan Evans

Copyright © 2015 Susan Evans

All rights reserved. This book or any portion thereof may not be reproduced or used in any manner whatsoever without the express written permission of the publisher except for the use of brief quotations in a book review.

Other popular books by Susan Evans

Quick & Easy Vegan Desserts Cookbook:
Over 80 delicious recipes for cakes, cupcakes, brownies, cookies, fudge, pies, candy, and so much more!

Vegetarian Slow Cooker Cookbook:
Over 75 recipes for meals, soups, stews, desserts, and sides

Quick & Easy Asian Vegetarian Cookbook:
Over 50 recipes for stir fries, rice, noodles, and appetizers

Vegetarian Mediterranean Cookbook:
Over 50 recipes for appetizers, salads, dips, and main dishes

The Vegetarian DASH Diet Cookbook:
Over 100 recipes for breakfast, lunch, dinner and sides!

Quick & Easy Vegan No-Bake Desserts Cookbook:
Over 75 delicious recipes for cookies, fudge, bars, and other tasty treats!

Quick & Easy Microwave Meals:
Over 50 recipes for breakfast, snacks, meals and desserts

Quick & Easy Vegetarian Rice Cooker Meals:
Over 50 recipes for breakfast, main dishes, and desserts

Halloween Cookbook:
80 Ghoulish recipes for appetizers, meals, drinks, and desserts

Free Bonus!

Would you like to receive one of my cookbooks for free? Just leave me on honest review on Amazon and I will send you a digital version of the cookbook of your choice! All you have to do is email me proof of your review and the desired cookbook and format to susan.evans.author@gmail.com. Thank you for your support, and have fun cooking!

INTRODUCTION 1

MEASUREMENT CONVERSIONS 2

VEGAN 3

Korean BBQ Burger *4*
Tex-Mex Vegan Burger *5*
Black Bean Burgers *6*
Smoky Black Bean Burgers *8*
Grilled Portobello Mushroom Burgers *9*
Spicy Black Bean and Corn Burgers *10*
Carrot Rice Nut Burger *11*
Mexican Bean Burgers *12*
Bean Barley Burgers *13*
Garbanzo Bean Burgers *14*

VEGETARIAN 15

Delicata Squash Burger Patties *16*
Italian Patties *17*
Monterey Jack Eggplant Burgers *18*
Portobello Mushroom Burger with Bruschetta *19*
Jamaican Bean Burgers *20*
Quinoa Black Bean Burgers *21*
Lentil Cakes *22*
Zucchini Patties *23*
Portobello Mushroom Burgers *24*
Spicy Black Bean Burger *25*
Carrot Burgers *26*
Butter Bean Burgers *27*

Black Bean Chili Burgers 28
Tofu Burgers 29
Mushroom Burgers 30
Chickpea Falafel Burgers 31
Brown Rice Burgers 32
Carrot Burgers 33
Nut and Chickpea Burgers 34
Portobello Burgers with Goat Cheese 36
Garbanzo Bean Patties 38
Tofu and Plantain Patties 39
Barley Black Bean Burgers 40
Mushroom Garlic Burger 41

THANK YOU 42

INTRODUCTION

Who doesn't love a succulent and juicy burger? Whether grilling at a summertime barbecue or flipping burger patties over your stove, creating delicious burgers doesn't always require meat. The following veggie burgers recipes offer a deliciously healthy (and tastier) alternative for vegetarians, vegans, and anyone just trying to eat healthier. Whether cooking for family or friends, everyone will love these mouth-watering burgers!

The following easy to create recipes will open the possibilities to veggie-based burgers that will tickle even the pickiest of taste buds. Each recipe is tried and true, and compiled to get the perfect hamburger experience without the meat! With more than 30 vegetarian and vegan* recipes, this book will change the way you think about burgers. So start the grill, and let's get cooking!

*To make all recipes vegan, you can substitute non-vegan ingredients with vegan versions of your favorite brand. Recommended substitutions:
1 egg=1 tablespoon flax to 3 tablespoons of almost-boiling water, whisked = ¼ cup avocado
Butter=vegan margarine=canola, sunflower, or olive oil
Cheeses=your favorite vegan cheese brand
Milk=soy, rice, or almond milk

MEASUREMENT CONVERSIONS

Liquid/Volume Measurements (approximate)

1 teaspoon = 1/6 fluid ounce (oz.) = 1/3 tablespoon = 5 ml

1 tablespoon = 1/2 fluid ounce (oz.) = 3 teaspoons = 15 ml

1 fluid ounce (oz.) = 2 tablespoons = 1/8 cup = 30 ml

1/4 cup = 2 fluid ounces (oz.) = 4 tablespoons = 60 ml

1/3 cup = 2⅔ fluid ounces (oz.) = 5 ⅓ tablespoons = 80 ml

1/2 cup = 4 fluid ounces (oz.) = 8 tablespoons = 120 ml

2/3 cup = 5⅓ fluid ounces (oz.) = 10⅔ tablespoons = 160 ml

3/4 cup = 6 fluid ounces (oz.) = 12 tablespoons = 180 ml

7/8 cup = 7 fluid ounces (oz.) = 14 tablespoons = 210 ml

1 cup = 8 fluid ounces (oz.) = 1/2 pint = 240 ml

1 pint = 16 fluid ounces (oz.) = 2 cups = 1/2 quart = 475 ml

1 quart = 4 cups = 32 fluid ounces (oz.) = 2 pints = 950 ml

1 liter = 1.055 quarts = 4.22 cups = 2.11 pints = 1000 ml

1 gallon = 4 quarts = 8 pints = 3.8 liters

Dry/Weight Measurements (approximate)

1 ounce (oz.) = 30 grams (g)

2 ounces (oz.) = 55 grams (g)

3 ounces (oz.) = 85 grams (g)

1/4 pound (lb.) = 4 ounces (oz.) = 125 grams (g)

1/2 pound (lb.) = 8 ounces (oz.) = 240 grams (g)

3/4 pound (lb.) = 12 ounces (oz.) = 375 grams (g)

1 pound (lb.) = 16 ounces (oz.) = 455 grams (g)

2 pounds (lbs.) = 32 ounces (oz.) = 910 grams (g)

1 kilogram (kg) = 2.2 pounds (lbs.) = 1000 gram (g)

VEGAN

Korean BBQ Burger

SERVINGS: 8
PREP TIME: 15 min.
TOTAL TIME: 30 min.

Ingredients

- 1 (15.5 ounce) can garbanzo beans, drained and mashed
- 8 fresh basil leaves, chopped
- 1/4 cup oat bran
- 1/4 cup quick cooking oats
- 1 cup cooked brown rice
- 1 (14 ounce) package firm tofu
- 5 tablespoons Korean barbeque sauce
- 1/2 teaspoon salt
- 1/2 teaspoon ground black pepper
- 3/4 teaspoon garlic powder
- 3/4 teaspoon dried sage
- 2 teaspoons vegetable oil

Instructions

1. Stir together mashed garbanzo beans and basil in a large bowl. Mix in oat bran, quick oats, and rice.
2. In a different bowl, mash tofu with your hands, squeezing as much water as possible. Drain and repeat until there is barely any water left.
3. Pour barbeque sauce over the tofu, and completely coat. Stir in the tofu with the garbanzo beans and oats. Season with salt, pepper, garlic powder, and sage. Mix until well blended.
4. Heat oil over medium-high heat in a large skillet.
5. Form patties out of the bean mix, and fry in hot oil for about 5 minutes on each side.
6. Serve on burger buns.

Tex-Mex Vegan Burger

SERVINGS: 6
PREP TIME: 15 min.
TOTAL TIME: 30 min. + refrigeration

Ingredients

- 1/3 cup of white long-grain rice
- 2 (15-ounce) cans of black beans, rinsed
- 1 medium shallot, chopped
- 6 slices of pickled jalapeño
- 1 tablespoon of barbecue sauce
- 1 teaspoon of chili powder
- 1/2 teaspoon of ground cumin
- 1 egg white
- Salt
- Black pepper
- 4 tablespoons of vegetable oil, divided
- 6 hamburger buns
- Desired condiments

Instructions

1. Cook rice according to package directions. Let cool.
2. Set aside 1/2 cup of beans. Pulse shallot, jalapeño, barbecue sauce, chili powder, cumin, and the rest of the beans in a blender or food processor until a chunky paste forms.
3. Transfer mix to a medium bowl and combine with egg white, rice, and reserved beans. Season with salt and pepper. Form into 6 equal patties. Cover and chill for 1 hour.
4. In a large skillet, heat 2 tablespoons of oil over medium heat. Working in batches of two patties and adding the rest of the oil in between batches, cook until done.
5. Serve with desired condiments on buns.

Black Bean Burgers

SERVINGS: 4
PREP TIME: 15 min.
TOTAL TIME: 35 min.

Ingredients

- 1 (15 ounce) can black beans, drained and rinsed
- 1/3 cup chopped sweet onion
- 1 tablespoon minced garlic
- 3 baby carrots, grated (optional)
- 1/4 cup minced green bell pepper (optional)
- 1 tablespoon corn-starch
- 1 tablespoon warm water
- 3 tablespoons chile-garlic sauce, or to taste
- 1 teaspoon chili powder
- 1 teaspoon ground cumin
- 1 teaspoon seafood seasoning
- 1/4 teaspoon salt
- 1/4 teaspoon ground black pepper
- 2 slices whole-wheat bread, torn into small crumbs
- 3/4 cup unbleached flour, or as needed

Instructions

1. Preheat oven to 350 degrees F (175 degrees C). Grease a baking sheet.
2. Mash black beans in a bowl. Mix in onion, garlic, carrots, and green bell pepper.
3. In a small bowl, whisk corn-starch, water, chile-garlic sauce, chili powder, cumin, seafood seasoning, salt, and black pepper together. Stir corn-starch mixture into black bean mixture.
4. Mix whole-wheat bread in bean mixture. Stir flour, 1/4 cup at a time, into bean mix until a sticky batter forms. Spoon 3/4-inch thick burger shape mounds of batter onto the prepared baking sheet.

5. Bake in the preheated oven for about 10 minutes on each side until cooked in the center and crisp in the outside.

Smoky Black Bean Burgers

SERVINGS: 4
PREP TIME: 15 min.
TOTAL TIME: 55 min.

Ingredients

- 1 tablespoon ground flax seed
- 3 tablespoons water
- 1 (15 ounce) can black beans - drained, rinsed, and mashed
- 1/4 cup panko bread crumbs
- 1 clove garlic, minced
- 1/2 teaspoon salt
- 1/2 tablespoon Worcestershire sauce
- 1/8 teaspoon liquid smoke flavoring cooking spray

Instructions

1. In a small bowl, combine ground flax seed and water. Let sit for about 5 minutes.
2. Combine flax mixture, black beans, panko bread crumbs, garlic, salt, Worcestershire sauce, and liquid smoke in a bowl until well mixed. Form batter into 4 patties and arrange on a plate.
3. Chill in refrigerator for about 30 minutes until set.
4. Spray skillet with cooking spray. Place patties over medium heat in skillet. Cook until browned, about 5 minutes on each side.

Grilled Portobello Mushroom Burgers

SERVINGS: 4
PREP TIME: 10 min.
TOTAL TIME: 20 min.

Ingredients

- 4 large Portobello mushroom caps (about 12 ounces total)
- 1/3 cup balsamic vinegar
- 1/2 cup water
- 1 tablespoon sugar
- 1 garlic clove, minced
- 1/4 teaspoon cayenne pepper (optional)
- 2 tablespoons olive oil
- 4 whole-wheat buns, toasted
- 4 slices tomato
- 4 slices red onion
- 2 Bibb lettuce leaves, halved

Instructions

1. Clean mushrooms with damp cloth and remove stems. Place in a dish, gill side up.
2. Prepare marinade in a small bowl by whisking together vinegar, water, sugar, garlic, cayenne pepper and olive oil. Drizzle marinade over mushrooms. Cover and leave in refrigerator for about 1 hour to marinate. Turn mushrooms over once.
3. Position cooking rack 4 to 6 inches from heat source. Preheat a gas grill or broiler.
4. Broil mushrooms, turning often, until tender, about 5 minutes on each side. Baste with marinade and avoid drying out. Use tongs and transfer mushrooms to a plate.
5. Place each mushroom on a bun and top with 1 tomato slice, 1 onion slice and 1/2 lettuce leaf.
6. Serve immediately.

Spicy Black Bean and Corn Burgers

SERVINGS: 4
PREP TIME: 15 min.
TOTAL TIME: 35 min

Ingredients

- 1 tablespoon olive oil
- 1 small onion, diced
- 2 cloves garlic, minced
- 1 jalapeno pepper, seeded and minced
- 1 teaspoon dried oregano
- 1/2 red bell pepper, diced
- 1 ear corn, kernels cut from cob
- 1 (15 ounce) can black beans, drained and rinsed
- 1/2 cup plain bread crumbs
- 4 teaspoons chili powder
- 1 tablespoon minced fresh cilantro
- 1/2 teaspoon ground cumin
- 1/2 teaspoon salt
- 1/2 cup all-purpose flour, or as needed
- 1 tablespoon olive oil, or as needed

Instructions

1. In a skillet, heat 1 tablespoon olive oil over medium heat. Cook and stir onion, garlic, jalapeno pepper, and oregano for 8 to 10 minutes or until onions are translucent. Mix in red bell pepper and corn into onion mix for 2 to 4 more minutes or until red bell pepper is tender.
2. Mash black beans in a large bowl.
3. Stir vegetable mixture, bread crumbs, chili powder, cilantro, cumin, and salt into mashed black beans. Divide mix into 4 patties and completely coat patties with flour.
4. In a skillet, heat 1 tablespoon olive oil over medium heat. Cook patties 5 to 8 minutes on each side, until browned.

Carrot Rice Nut Burger

SERVINGS: 20
PREP TIME: 10 min.
TOTAL TIME: 1 hour

Ingredients

- 3 cups uncooked brown rice
- 6 cups water
- 1 cup toasted cashews
- 1 pound toasted unsalted sunflower seeds
- 1 sweet onion, chopped
- 6 carrots, chopped
- 1 tablespoon extra-virgin olive oil
- Salt, to taste

Instructions

1. Bring the rice and water to a boil in a large pot. Reduce heat to low, cover, and simmer for 45 minutes.
2. Preheat the grill for high heat.
3. With a food processor, finely blend the toasted cashews and sunflower seeds. Transfer to a large bowl.
4. In the food processor, pulse the onion and carrots until finely blende and mix with the ground nuts. Place cooked rice and olive oil in the food processor, and pulse until smooth. Mix into the bowl and season with salt.
5. Form the mix into patties.
6. Oil the grill grate and grill the patties 6 to 8 minutes on each side, until nicely browned. (You can also fry them in a skillet instead).

Mexican Bean Burgers

SERVINGS: 8
PREP TIME: 10 min.
TOTAL TIME: 25 min.

Ingredients

- 1 carrot, sliced
- 1 (15 ounce) can kidney beans
- 1/2 cup chopped green bell pepper
- 1/2 cup chopped onion
- 2 cups salsa
- 1 cup dried bread crumbs
- 1/2 cup whole wheat flour
- 1/2 teaspoon ground black pepper
- Salt, to taste
- 1 pinch chili powder

Instructions

1. Place carrot in a bowl, filling with 1/4 inch of water. Cover with plastic wrap, and cook in microwave for 2 minutes, or until soft. Drain the water.
2. Mash beans and steamed carrot in a large bowl. Add in green pepper, onion, salsa, bread crumbs, and whole wheat flour. Season with salt, black pepper, and chili powder.
3. Add flour to create a stiffer mixture, or add more salsa if the mix is too firm. Form into 8 patties, and place on a greased baking sheet.
4. Heat a large skillet over medium-high heat, and coat with cooking spray. Fry patties for about 8 minutes on each side, or until firm and brown.

Bean Barley Burgers

SERVINGS: 8
PREP TIME: 10 min.
TOTAL TIME: 25 min.

Ingredients

- 1/2 teaspoon garlic powder
- 2 cups kidney beans cooked
- 1/2 cup wheat germ
- 1 tablespoon olive oil
- 1/2 cup onion chopped
- 3 garlic cloves, minced
- 1 teaspoon sea salt
- 1/2 teaspoon sage
- 1/2 teaspoon celery seed, ground
- 2 cups whole hull-less barley, cooked

Instructions

1. Cook beans and barley according to package instructions until soft. Mash beans and barley together.
2. Fry onion and garlic in oil until golden. Add bean/barley mix along with spices and wheat germ. Stir to combine.
3. Form into 4" patties and fry on medium heat until brown on both sides.
4. Makes about 8 burgers.

Garbanzo Bean Burgers

SERVINGS: 4
PREP TIME: 15 min.
TOTAL TIME: 1 hour

Ingredients

- 1 (15 ounce) can garbanzo beans (chickpeas), rinsed and drained
- 1 red bell pepper, finely chopped
- 1 carrot, grated
- 3 cloves garlic, minced
- 1 red chile pepper, seeded and minced
- 2 tablespoons chopped fresh cilantro
- 1 tablespoon tahini paste
- salt and black pepper, to taste
- 1 teaspoon olive oil (optional)

Instructions

1. Place garbanzo beans (chickpeas) in a blender or food processor with bell pepper, carrot, garlic, red chile pepper, cilantro, tahini, salt, and pepper. Cover and pulse 5 times. Scrape the sides and pulse until mixed. If the mix is dry, add olive oil. Refrigerate for 30 minutes.
2. Preheat oven to 350 degrees F (175 degrees C).
3. Prepare a baking sheet with parchment paper or lightly grease with cooking spray. Shape the garbanzo bean burger mix into patties.
4. Bake 20 minutes. Flip and bake for 10 minutes more or until evenly browned.

VEGETARIAN

Delicata Squash Burger Patties

SERVINGS: 4
PREP TIME: 15 min.
TOTAL TIME: 1 hour 15 min.

Ingredients

- 1 delicata squash, halved lengthwise and seeded
- 1 tablespoon olive oil (optional)
- salt and ground black pepper to taste
- 2 tablespoons butter
- 1 shallot, minced
- 1 clove garlic, minced
- 6 sun-dried tomatoes, chopped
- 1 cup bread crumbs, or more if needed
- 1 egg, beaten
- 1/4 cup grated Parmesan cheese
- 1/4 cup vegetable oil, or as needed

Instructions

1. Preheat an oven to 475 degrees F (245 degrees C). Place squash on a baking sheet and drizzle with olive oil. Season with salt and pepper. Bake in the oven for about 45 minutes or until tender. Remove and cool. Cut into cubes.
2. In a skillet, heat butter over medium heat. Cook and stir shallot and garlic in the melted butter for 5 to 10 minutes until shallot is transparent. Add sun-dried tomatoes. Cook until softened, about 2 to 3 minutes. Mash squash cubes into shallot mixture until smooth. Remove from heat, transfer to a bowl, and cool for 2 to 3 minutes.
3. Stir bread crumbs, egg, and Parmesan cheese into squash mix. Add more bread crumbs it's too sticky and season with salt and pepper. Shape into 4 patties.
4. In a large frying pan, heat vegetable oil over medium-high heat. Cook patties 4 to 5 minutes on each side until browned.

Italian Patties

SERVINGS: 16
PREP TIME: 20 min.
TOTAL TIME: 40 min.

Ingredients

- 2 tablespoons vegetable oil
- 3/4 cup uncooked brown rice
- 1 1/2 cups red lentils
- 6 cups water
- 1 teaspoon salt
- 2 eggs
- 2 1/2 cups dry bread crumbs
- 1 1/2 cups grated Parmesan cheese
- 2 teaspoons dried basil
- 1 1/2 teaspoons garlic powder
- 3 tablespoons vegetable oil

Instructions

1. Heat 2 tablespoons of oil in a large saucepan. Stir in brown rice and cook until golden brown. Add lentils, water, and salt. Bring to a boil then reduce heat to low. Cover and cook about 40 minutes or until the water has absorbed and the rice is tender. Add more water if needed, the mix should be thick. Remove from heat and let cool a bit.
2. Place rice mix in a food processor or blender. Add eggs, bread crumbs, Parmesan cheese, basil, and garlic powder. Process until well combined, and the texture is like ground meat.
3. Form into 1/4 to 1/2 inch thick patties. Heat 3 tablespoons oil in a large skillet. Fry patties until browned, around 2 to 3 minutes on each side. Drain on paper towels. Repeat until all patties have cooked.
4. Let cool and serve.

Monterey Jack Eggplant Burgers

SERVINGS: 6
PREP TIME: 7 min.
TOTAL TIME: 20 min.

Ingredients

- 1 eggplant, peeled and sliced into 3/4 inch rounds
- 1 tablespoon margarine
- 6 slices Monterey Jack cheese
- 6 hamburger buns, split
- 6 leaves lettuce
- 6 slices tomato
- 1/2 onion, sliced
- 1/2 cup dill pickle slices
- 1 (20 ounce) bottle ketchup
- 3 tablespoons mayonnaise
- 2 tablespoons prepared yellow mustard

Instructions

1. Place eggplant slices on a microwaveable plate. Cook in microwave for about 5 minutes, or until the center is cooked.
2. In a large skillet, melt margarine over medium-high heat.
3. Fry eggplant slices until toasted lightly on each side. Place a slice of cheese on each slice and cook until cheese has melted.
4. Remove from skillet and place eggplant on hamburger buns. Top with lettuce, tomato, onion, and pickles, and dress with ketchup, mayonnaise and mustard; or any other desired toppings.

Portobello Mushroom Burger with Bruschetta

SERVINGS: 2
PREP TIME: 20 min.
TOTAL TIME: 1 hour + refrigeration

Ingredients

- 8 Roma (plum) tomatoes, diced
- 1/3 cup chopped fresh basil
- 1/4 cup shredded Parmesan cheese
- 1 tablespoon balsamic vinegar
- 2 cloves garlic, minced
- 1 teaspoon olive oil
- 1/2 teaspoon kosher salt
- 1/2 teaspoon ground black pepper
- 2 large Portobello mushroom caps, stems removed
- 2 tablespoons shredded horseradish Cheddar cheese, or to taste (optional)
- 2 Kaiser rolls, split

Instructions

1. In a bowl, combine the Roma tomatoes, basil, Parmesan cheese, balsamic vinegar, garlic, olive oil, kosher salt, and black pepper. Refrigerate for 1 to 2 hours to marinate.
2. Preheat grill for medium heat and lightly oil the grate.
3. Grill Portobello mushrooms with gill sides up on an upper rack of the grill for about 15 minutes, or until hot and juicy. Spoon tomato mix into mushrooms and cover the entire cap. Continue grilling for another 15 to 20 minutes or until heated through.
4. Top with Cheddar cheese if desired, and grill until cheese has melted; about 1 to 2 minutes.
5. Serve on Kaiser Rolls.

Jamaican Bean Burgers

SERVINGS: 6
PREP TIME: 10 min.
TOTAL TIME: 30 min

Ingredients

- 2 tablespoons olive oil
- 2 1/4 cups chopped onion
- 3 cloves garlic, minced
- 1 habanero pepper, chopped
- 1 1/2 tablespoons grated fresh ginger root
- 1 teaspoon salt
- 3/4 teaspoon ground allspice
- 3/4 teaspoon ground nutmeg
- 2 1/4 cups cooked black beans, rinsed and drained
- 2 1/4 cups cooked long-grain white rice
- 2 1/2 cups dry bread crumbs
- 6 hamburger buns, split

Instructions

1. In a large skillet, heat 1 tablespoon of olive oil over medium heat. Add onions and garlic. Cook and stir for a few minutes. Mix in habanero pepper and cook until tender. Remove from heat and transfer to a bowl.
2. Pour in the beans, rice and bread crumbs. Season with ginger, salt, allspice and nutmeg. Mix well with your hands and form into 6 patties.
3. Heat remaining oil in a large skillet over medium-high heat. Fry the patties for about 10 minutes, or until golden on each side.
4. Serve on buns with your favorite toppings.

Quinoa Black Bean Burgers

SERVINGS: 5
PREP TIME: 15 min.
TOTAL TIME: 35 min.

Ingredients

- 1 (15 ounce) can black beans, rinsed and drained
- 1/4 cup quinoa
- 1/2 cup water
- 1/2 cup bread crumbs
- 1/4 cup minced yellow bell pepper
- 2 tablespoons minced onion
- 1 large clove garlic, minced
- 1 1/2 teaspoons ground cumin
- 1/2 teaspoon salt
- 1 teaspoon hot pepper sauce
- 1 egg
- 3 tablespoons olive oil

Instructions

1. Add water and quinoa to a saucepan and bring water to boil. Reduce heat to medium-low and cover. Simmer until quinoa is tender and water is absorbed, about 15 to 20 minutes.
2. Mash the black beans with a fork leaving some whole black beans in this mixture.
3. With your hands, combine the quinoa, bread crumbs, bell pepper, onion, garlic, cumin, salt, hot pepper sauce, and egg with the black beans.
4. Form black bean mix into 5 patties.
5. Heat the olive oil in a large skillet. Cook patties in the hot oil until heated throughout, around 2 to 3 minutes per side.

Lentil Cakes

SERVINGS: 8
PREP TIME: 30 min.
TOTAL TIME: 1 hour

Ingredients

- 1 cup dry brown lentils
- 2 1/2 cups water
- 1/4 cup milk
- 1 cup wheat and barley nugget cereal
- 1 (1 ounce) envelope dry onion soup mix
- 1/2 teaspoon poultry seasoning
- 2 eggs, beaten
- 1/2 cup chopped walnuts
- 1 cup seasoned dry bread crumbs
- 2 tablespoons vegetable oil

Instructions

1. In a saucepan, combine lentils and water; and bring to a boil. Cover, reduce heat to low, and simmer until tender, about 30 minutes. Drain the water.
2. Combine the cooked lentils, milk, wheat and barley cereal, eggs and walnuts in a large bowl.
3. Season with onion soup mix and poultry seasoning. Mix well with your hands and let stand for 30 minutes, or refrigerate overnight. Heat oil over medium heat in a large skillet.
4. With an ice cream scoop, scoop out balls of the lentil mix. Drop scoops into bread crumbs, and coat while shaping into patties. Fry in the hot skillet until browned on both sides, about 10 minutes total, depending on patty thickness.

Zucchini Patties

SERVINGS: 4
PREP TIME: 10 min.
TOTAL TIME: 30 min.

Ingredients

- 2 cups grated zucchini
- 2 eggs, beaten
- 1/4 cup chopped onion
- 1/2 cup all-purpose flour
- 1/2 cup grated Parmesan cheese
- 1/2 cup shredded mozzarella cheese
- Salt, to taste
- 2 tablespoons vegetable oil

Instructions

1. Combine zucchini, eggs, onion, flour, Parmesan cheese, mozzarella cheese, and salt in a medium bowl. Stir to distribute ingredients evenly.
2. Heat some oil in a skillet over medium-high heat.
3. Drop zucchini mixture by large tablespoonfuls, cooking for a few minutes on each side until it is golden.

Portobello Mushroom Burgers

SERVINGS: 4
PREP TIME: 15 min.
TOTAL TIME: 35 min.

Ingredients

- 4 Portobello mushroom caps
- 1/4 cup balsamic vinegar
- 2 tablespoons olive oil
- 1 teaspoon dried basil
- 1 teaspoon dried oregano
- 1 tablespoon minced garlic
- salt and pepper, to taste
- 4 (1 ounce) slices provolone cheese

Instructions

1. Place mushrooms in a shallow dish smooth side up. Whisk together vinegar, oil, basil, oregano, garlic, salt, and pepper in a small bowl. Pour on top of the mushrooms. Let stand for 15 minutes and turn twice.
2. Preheat grill for medium-high heat. Brush grate with oil. Place mushrooms on the grill and reserve marinade for basting. Grill for 5 to 8 minutes on each side, or until tender; brushing frequently with marinade. Top with cheese during last 2 minutes of grilling.

Spicy Black Bean Burger

SERVINGS: 4
PREP TIME: 15 min.
TOTAL TIME: 30 min.

Ingredients

- 1 (16-ounce) can of black beans, drained, rinsed
- 1/2 green bell pepper, cut into slices
- 1/2 onion, cut into wedges
- 3 cloves of garlic, peeled
- 1 egg
- 1 tablespoon of chili powder
- 1 tablespoon of cumin
- 1 teaspoon of hot sauce
- 1/2 cup of bread crumbs

Instructions

1. Preheat oven to 375 degrees F (190 degrees C).
2. Mash black beans into a paste in a medium bowl.
3. In a food processor or blender, chop bell pepper, onion, and garlic, then stir into mashed beans.
4. Combine egg, chili powder, cumin, and hot sauce in a small bowl.
5. Stir egg mix into mashed beans. Mix in bread crumbs. Divide and form into 4 patties.
6. Lightly oil a baking sheet. Place patties on a baking sheet and bake for 10 minutes on each side.
7. Serve.

Carrot Burgers

SERVINGS: 12
PREP TIME: 15 min.
TOTAL TIME: 40 min.

Ingredients

- 2 cups shredded carrots
- 2 eggs
- 1/2 cup mayonnaise
- 1 medium onion, minced
- 2 tablespoons olive oil
- 1 clove garlic, chopped
- salt and pepper to taste
- 6 cups soft bread crumbs
- 4 cups whole wheat flake cereal, crumbled

Instructions

1. Preheat oven to 375 degrees F (190 degrees C). Place carrots in a bowl and cover. Heat in the microwave for 2 to 3 minutes, or until tender.
2. Mix and stir together the eggs, mayonnaise, onion, olive oil, garlic, salt, pepper, and carrots in a large bowl. Add and combine in bread crumbs until blended evenly. Shape into 12 patties. Pour cereal on a plate, and coat patties in the cereal.
3. Place patties on a greased baking sheet and bake for 25 to 30 minutes, turning once or until golden brown.

Butter Bean Burgers

SERVINGS: 4
PREP TIME: 15 min.
TOTAL TIME: 25 min.

Ingredients

- 1 (15 ounce) can butter beans, drained
- 1 small onion, chopped
- 1 tablespoon finely chopped jalapeno pepper
- 6 saltine crackers, crushed
- 1 egg, beaten
- 1/2 cup shredded Cheddar cheese
- 1/4 teaspoon garlic powder
- salt and pepper, to taste
- 1/4 cup vegetable oil

Instructions

1. Mash butter beans in a medium bowl. Add in onion, jalapeno pepper, crushed crackers, egg, cheese, garlic powder, salt, and pepper. Mix well and divide into 4 equal parts. Shape into patties.
2. In a large skillet, heat oil over medium-high heat, enough oil to reach 1/4 inch in depth. Fry patties for about 5 minutes, turning once until each side is golden.

Black Bean Chili Burgers

SERVINGS: 4
PREP TIME: 15 min.
TOTAL TIME: 35 min.

Ingredients

- 1 (16 ounce) can black beans, drained and rinsed
- 1/2 green bell pepper, cut into 2 inch pieces
- 1/2 onion, cut into wedges
- 3 cloves garlic, peeled
- 1 egg
- 1 tablespoon chili powder
- 1 tablespoon cumin
- 1 teaspoon Thai chili sauce or hot sauce
- 1/2 cup bread crumbs

Instructions

1. If you are grilling, preheat outdoor grill for high heat, and oil a sheet of aluminum foil lightly. If baking, preheat oven to 375 degrees F (190 degrees C), and lightly oil a baking sheet.
2. Mash black beans with a fork in a medium bowl until thick and pasty.
3. In a blender or food processor, finely chop bell pepper, onion, and garlic. Combine this mix with the mashed beans.
4. In a small bowl, stir egg, chili powder, cumin, and chili sauce. Stir this mix into mashed beans.
5. Mix in bread crumbs until the mix is sticky. Divide and shape into four patties.
6. If grilling, place patties on foil, and grill for about 8 minutes on each side. If baking, place patties on baking sheet, and bake about 10 minutes on each side.

Tofu Burgers

SERVINGS: 6
PREP TIME: 15 min.
TOTAL TIME: 30 min.

Ingredients

- 1 (12 ounce) package firm tofu
- 2 teaspoons vegetable oil
- 1 small onion, chopped
- 1 celery, chopped
- 1 egg, beaten
- 1/4 cup shredded Cheddar cheese
- salt and pepper to taste
- 1/2 cup vegetable oil, for frying

Instructions

1. In a small skillet, heat 2 teaspoons of vegetable oil.
2. Sauté the onion and celery until lightly browned and soft. Place in a medium bowl and set aside.
3. Squeeze out excess water from tofu. Chop finely and place in bowl with onion and celery. Combine with egg, cheese, salt and pepper until. Heat a large skillet over medium-high heat and pour in 1/2 cup vegetable oil, or enough to be 1/4 inch deep.
4. Drop tofu mixture into pan in 6 equal parts. Flatten to form patties. Fry for 5 to 7 minutes on each side, until golden.

Mushroom Burgers

SERVINGS: 6
PREP TIME: 20 min.
TOTAL TIME: 30 min.

Ingredients

- 1 pound fresh mushrooms, sliced
- 1 large onion, minced
- 2 slices white bread, finely diced
- 2 tablespoons oyster sauce
- 1 egg
- Salt, to taste
- ground black pepper, to taste

Instructions

1. Place large skillet over medium heat and spray with cooking spray. Add mushrooms and onions, cooking for about 4 minutes, stirring throughout. Stir in bread cubes and oyster sauce and cook another 1 minute.
2. Remove mix from pan, and set aside to cool. Wipe the pan clean.
3. Beat the egg and combine into mushroom mixture. Season to taste with salt and pepper.
4. Place the skillet over medium heat and coat with cooking spray.
5. Divide the mix into 6 equal amounts and mix into skillet. Cook until brown on one side. Flip and brown other side.
6. Serve.

Chickpea Falafel Burgers

SERVINGS: 4
PREP TIME: 15 min.
TOTAL TIME: 25 min.

Ingredients

- 1 tablespoon vegetable oil
- 2 green onions, chopped
- 3/4 cup diced fresh mushrooms
- 3 cloves garlic, chopped
- 1 (15.5 ounce) can garbanzo beans, with liquid
- 1 1/2 tablespoons chopped fresh cilantro
- 1 1/2 teaspoons minced fresh parsley
- 1 1/2 tablespoons curry powder
- 1/2 teaspoon ground cumin
- 1/2 cup dry bread crumbs
- 2 egg whites
- 2 tablespoons vegetable oil, or as needed

Instructions

1. In a large skillet, heat 1 tablespoon of oil over medium-high heat. Add green onions and mushrooms. Cook until tender, frequently stirring.
2. In a blender or food processor, combine the garbanzo beans (along with the liquid) and garlic. Blend until smooth. Transfer to a medium bowl and stir in the mushrooms and onions.
3. Mix in cilantro, parsley, curry powder and cumin. Add bread crumbs and egg whites, mixing until well blended.
4. Over medium heat in a large skillet, heat enough oil to cover the bottom. Form bean mix into 4 balls, and flatten into patties. Fry each for about 5 minutes until browned on each side.

Brown Rice Burgers

SERVINGS: 12
PREP/TOTAL TIME: 35 min.

Ingredients

- 2 cups cooked brown rice
- 1/2 cup parsley, chopped
- 1 cup carrot, finely grated
- 1/2 cup onion, finely chopped
- 1 clove garlic, minced
- 1 teaspoon salt
- 1/4 teaspoon ground black pepper
- 2 eggs, beaten
- 1/2 cup whole wheat flour
- 2 tablespoons vegetable oil for cooking

Instructions

1. In a medium mixing bowl, combine all ingredients except oil. Form mix into 12 patties, firmly pressing with hands.
2. Add vegetable oil to a skillet and heat over medium heat. Cook patties until brown, about 4-5 minutes per side, turning once.

Carrot Burgers

SERVINGS: 12
PREP TIME: 15 min.
TOTAL TIME: 35 min.

Ingredients

- 2 cups shredded carrots
- 2 eggs
- 1/2 cup mayonnaise
- 1 medium onion, minced
- 2 tablespoons olive oil
- 1 clove garlic, chopped
- salt and pepper, to taste
- 6 cups soft bread crumbs
- 4 cups whole wheat flake cereal, crumbled

Instructions

1. Preheat oven to 375 degrees F (190 degrees C).
2. Place carrots in a bowl. Cover and heat in the microwave until tender, about 2 to 3 minutes.
3. In a large bowl, mix the eggs, mayonnaise, onion, olive oil, garlic, salt, pepper, and carrots. Mix in bread crumbs until well blended. Shape into 12 patties. Pour cereal on plate, and dip patties to coat.
4. Place patties on a greased baking sheet. Bake for 25 to 30 minutes turning once in oven, until golden brown.

Nut and Chickpea Burgers

SERVINGS: 2
PREP TIME: 10 min.
TOTAL TIME: 25 min.

Ingredients

- 1/2 cup finely chopped walnuts
- 1/2 cup unsalted sunflower seeds
- 1 cup canned chickpeas, drained
- 1/4 cup diced red onion
- 1 beaten egg
- 1 tablespoon chopped fresh parsley
- 1/4 teaspoon fresh ground black pepper
- 1 tablespoon salt-free herb seasoning blend
- 2 tablespoons olive oil
- 2 slices mild Cheddar cheese
- 1 pita bread round
- 1/4 cup prepared Ranch salad dressing
- 2 leaves romaine lettuce
- 1 medium tomato, thinly sliced
- 1/2 avocado - peeled, pitted and sliced

Instructions

1. Place walnuts and sunflower seeds in a skillet over medium heat. Cook for about 5 minutes until lightly toasted and fragrant, occasionally stirring.
2. In a medium bowl, mash garbanzo beans with a fork, or chop in a blender. Stir in onion, egg, parsley, and toasted nuts. Season with pepper and seasoning blend and mix well.
3. Heat olive oil in a skillet over medium heat.
4. Divide the bean mix into 2 patties, and fry in hot oil for about 3 minutes on each side, or until heated through and browned. Place a slice of cheese over each patty, and remove from heat.
5. Place pita round in the same dry skillet as the nuts were in, and heat for about 1 minute on each side.

6. Cut round in half and spread ranch dressing inside of each. Line pockets with romaine leaves, and place a cheesy patty on each. Top with sliced tomato and avocado.
7. Serve with tortilla or potato chips.

Portobello Burgers with Goat Cheese

SERVINGS: 4
PREP TIME: 10 min.
TOTAL TIME: 1 hour

Ingredients

- 2 medium beets
- 1/4 cup olive oil
- 2 tablespoons balsamic vinegar
- 1 teaspoon dried rosemary
- 2 cloves garlic, minced and divided
- 4 Portobello mushroom caps
- 1/2 cup goat cheese
- 4 sandwich buns, split and toasted
- 1 1/2 cups baby spinach leaves
- 3 tablespoons mayonnaise
- 2 cloves garlic, minced
- 2 limes, juiced

Instructions

1. Preheat oven to 400 degrees F (200 degrees C).
2. Cut tops off the beets and place them in a dish with enough water to cover the bottom. Roast in the preheated oven for about 40 to 50 minutes, or until you can easily pierce them with a knife. Remove and refrigerate until cool. Slice and set aside.
3. Preheat oven's broiler and set rack to the second level from the heat source.
4. In a bowl, whisk olive oil, balsamic vinegar, rosemary, and 2 cloves minced garlic together. Spread half of this mix over the ribbed side of the Portobello mushroom caps. Arrange mushrooms on a baking sheet with the ribbed sides facing upwards. Broil the mushrooms 5 to 7 minutes or until tender, avoid burning the garlic.
5. Flip mushrooms and brush the remaining olive oil mixture over the tops of the caps. Return to the oven and broil until tender, about 5 minutes. Spread equal amounts of the goat cheese on one half of each of the sandwich rolls. Top each with sliced beets and spinach.

6. Whisk mayonnaise, garlic, and lime juice together in a bowl. Spread evenly over the remaining halves of sandwich rolls and top with one mushroom cap. Bring the two halves together and serve.

Garbanzo Bean Patties

SERVINGS: 12
PREP TIME: 15 min.
TOTAL TIME: 3 hours

Ingredients

- 1 (16 ounce) package dry garbanzo beans (chickpeas)
- 1 onion, chopped
- 1 tablespoon dried thyme
- salt and pepper to taste
- 2 1/2 cups dry bread cubes
- 2 eggs, beaten
- 4 tablespoons vegetable oil

Instructions

1. Place garbanzo beans with 12 cups water in a large pot. Cook over medium heat for 2 1/2 to 3 hours, or until tender. Check occasionally, and add more water if needed.
2. In a blender blend small batches of the garbanzo beans on chop or blend setting, until mix is a paste. Add onions, thyme, salt and pepper to the mixture, mixing well.
3. Add bread cubes and egg, and mix well. Form mixture into patties.
4. Heat oil in a large skillet over medium heat. Fry patties until each side is golden brown.

Tofu and Plantain Patties

SERVINGS: 5
PREP TIME: 15 min.
TOTAL TIME: 30 min.

Ingredients

- 1 1/4 cups cubed tofu
- 1 1/4 cups chopped zucchini
- 1 plantain, peeled and sliced
- 1/2 cup canned sliced mushrooms
- 1/2 cup sun-dried tomatoes
- 1/2 cup bread crumbs
- 1/4 cup black olives
- 1 large clove garlic, roughly chopped
- 1 tablespoon butter, or as needed

Instructions

1. In a blender or food processor, blend tofu, zucchini, plantain, mushrooms, sun-dried tomatoes, bread crumbs, olives, and garlic until well mixed and thick. Form into 5 patties.
2. Heat butter over medium heat in a skillet. Cook patties, pressing lightly with a spatula in the hot butter, 3 to 5 minutes on each side until browned.

Barley Black Bean Burgers

SERVINGS: 4
PREP TIME: 15 min.
TOTAL TIME: 30 min.

Ingredients

- 1/2 cup quick-cooking barley
- 1 cup water
- 1 (16 ounce) can black beans, drained and rinsed
- 1 cup shredded Cheddar cheese
- 1 cup mushrooms, minced
- 1/2 onion, minced
- 1/2 red bell pepper, minced
- 1/4 cup fresh parsley, minced
- 2 large eggs
- 3 cloves garlic, minced
- salt and ground black pepper, to taste
- 1/2 cup bread crumbs, or as needed

Instructions

1. Preheat outdoor grill on high heat and lightly oil the grate. Grease a sheet of aluminum foil with oil.
2. In a saucepan, bring barley and water to a boil. Cover, reduce heat to low, and simmer for 10 to 15 minutes or until the barley is tender.
3. In a large bowl, mash black beans with a fork until thick. Stir barley, Cheddar cheese, mushrooms, onion, red bell pepper, parsley, eggs, garlic, salt, and black pepper into mashed black beans.
4. Mix bread crumbs into bean mixture until a sticky batter forms that holds together. Divide batter into 4 to 6 patties and place on prepared aluminum foil.
5. Grill patties on the aluminum foil for about 8 minutes on each side.

Mushroom Garlic Burger

SERVINGS: 6
PREP TIME: 15 min.
TOTAL TIME: 45 min.

Ingredients

- 2 tablespoons olive oil
- 3 (8 ounce) packages sliced fresh mushrooms
- 1/2 onion, finely chopped
- 4 cloves garlic, minced
- 1 teaspoon salt
- 1/2 teaspoon black pepper
- 1/2 teaspoon dried oregano
- 2/3 cup rolled oats
- 3/4 cup dry bread crumbs
- 2 eggs, beaten
- 1/2 cup freshly shredded Parmigiano-Reggiano cheese
- 2 tablespoons olive oil

Instructions

1. In a large skillet, heat 2 tablespoons olive oil over medium heat. Add mushrooms, onion, and garlic; season with salt, black pepper, and oregano. Cook and stir until mushrooms about 10 minutes until the juice has almost evaporated. Transfer mushrooms to a cutting board and cut into small chunks. Transfer to a large bowl.
2. Mix in rolled oats and bread crumbs. Add salt and black pepper to taste. Stir Parmigiano-Reggiano cheese and eggs into the mixture. Let stand for about 15 minutes or when the excess liquid has been absorbed. Moisten hands with water or vegetable oil and form around 1/4 cup of mixture into burgers.
3. In a skillet, heat remaining 2 tablespoons olive oil over medium heat. Fry burgers for about 5 to 6 minutes until browned and cooked through.

THANK YOU

Thank you for checking out the Veggie Burger Cookbook. I hope you enjoyed these recipes as much as I have. I am always looking for feedback on how to improve, so if you have any questions, suggestions, or comments please send me an email at susan.evans.author@gmail.com. Also, if you enjoyed the book would you consider leaving on honest review? As a new author, they help me out in a big way. Thanks again, and have fun cooking!

Other popular books by Susan Evans

Quick & Easy Vegan Desserts Cookbook:
Over 80 delicious recipes for cakes, cupcakes, brownies, cookies, fudge, pies, candy, and so much more!

Vegetarian Slow Cooker Cookbook:
Over 75 recipes for meals, soups, stews, desserts, and sides

Quick & Easy Asian Vegetarian Cookbook:
Over 50 recipes for stir fries, rice, noodles, and appetizers

Vegetarian Mediterranean Cookbook:
Over 50 recipes for appetizers, salads, dips, and main dishes

The Vegetarian DASH Diet Cookbook:
Over 100 recipes for breakfast, lunch, dinner and sides!

Quick & Easy Vegan No-Bake Desserts Cookbook:
Over 75 delicious recipes for cookies, fudge, bars, and other tasty treats!

Quick & Easy Microwave Meals:
Over 50 recipes for breakfast, snacks, meals and desserts

Quick & Easy Vegetarian Rice Cooker Meals:
Over 50 recipes for breakfast, main dishes, and desserts

Halloween Cookbook:
80 Ghoulish recipes for appetizers, meals, drinks, and desserts

Printed in Great Britain
by Amazon